Early Maths
Shapes

There are many shapes around us. Let us learn to identify them.

CIRCLE

TRIANGLE

RECTANGLE

ARROW

SQUARE

STAR

DIAMOND

HEART

CROSS

HEXAGON

PENTAGON

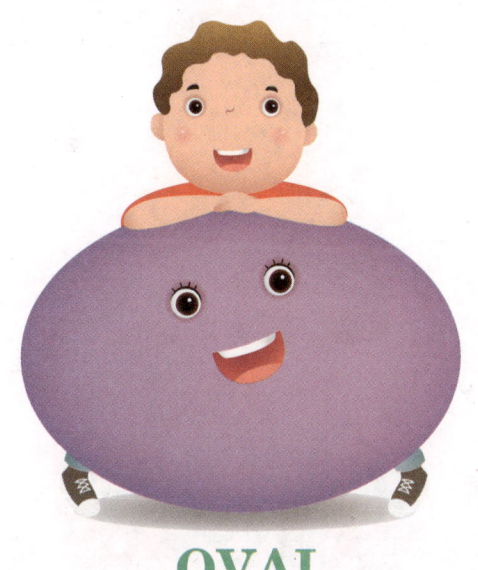

OVAL

Trace the circle and colour it.

Colour all the objects that are in the shape of circles.

Trace the triangle and colour it.

Colour all the objects that are in the shape of triangles.

Trace the square and colour it.

Square

Colour all the objects that are in the shape of squares.

Rectangle

Trace the rectangle and colour it.

10

Which shape does the train look like the most? Choose the correct option.

Square ☐

Rectangle ☐

Triangle ☐

Oval ☐

Can you draw some objects that look like these shapes? Draw one or more objects for each shape.

Circle

Triangle

Trace the shape and colour the hippo.

Trace the shape and colour the giraffe.

Oval

Trace and colour the oval. Try to draw the shape on your own.

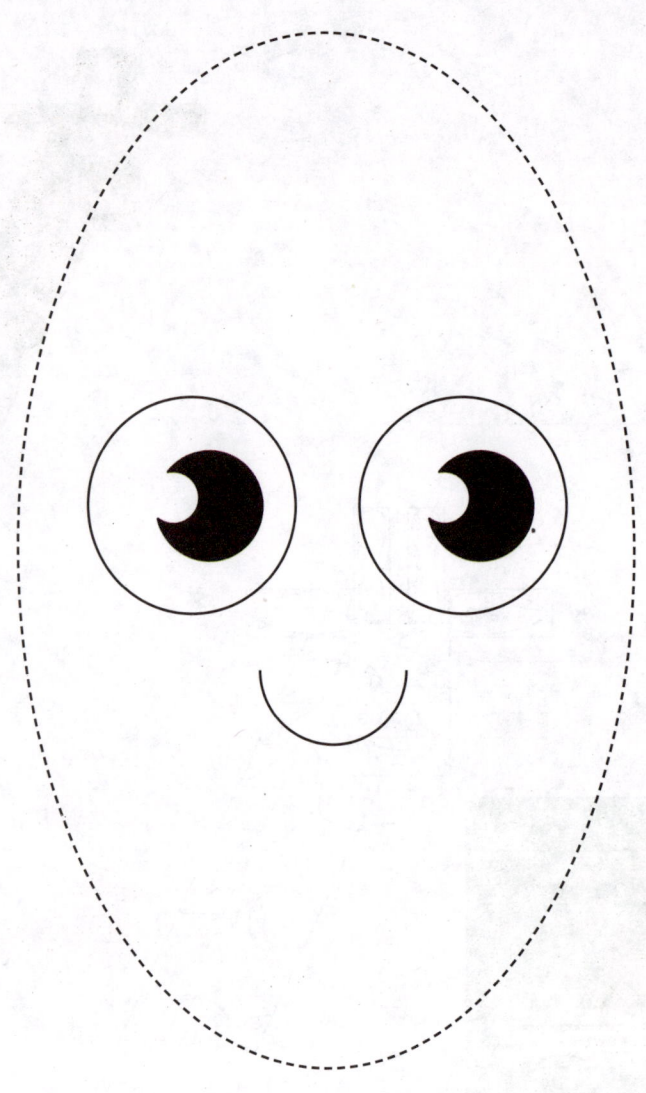

16

Trace the ovals and colour the footprints of Bruno the dog.

17

Trace and colour the rhombus. Try to draw the shape on your own.

Rhombus

18

Mark the object(s) in the shape of a rhombus with an arrow (→).

Trace, colour and draw a semicircle.

Trace the shape and colour the frog.

21

Trace the dots and try to make the shape on your own.

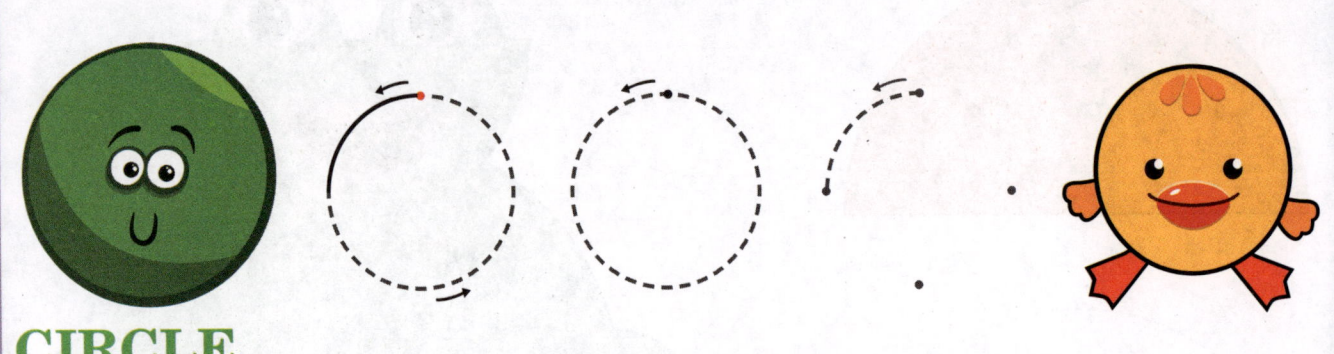

CIRCLE

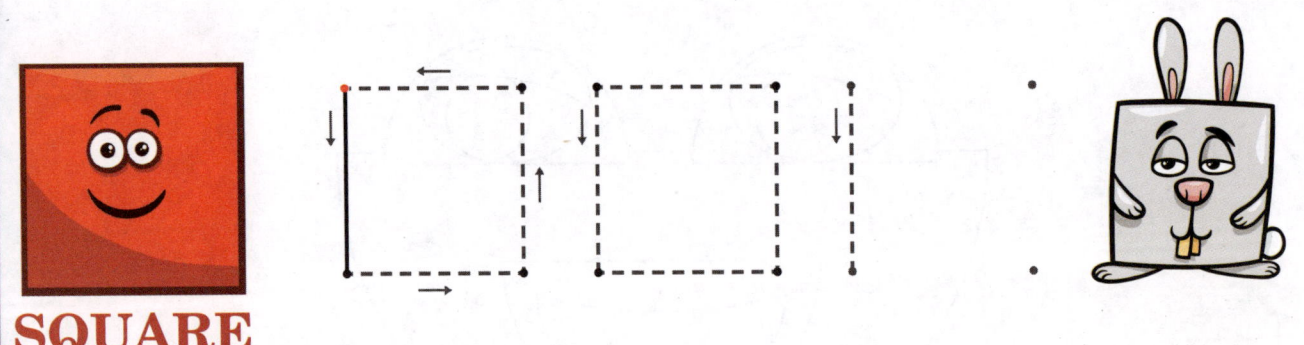

SQUARE

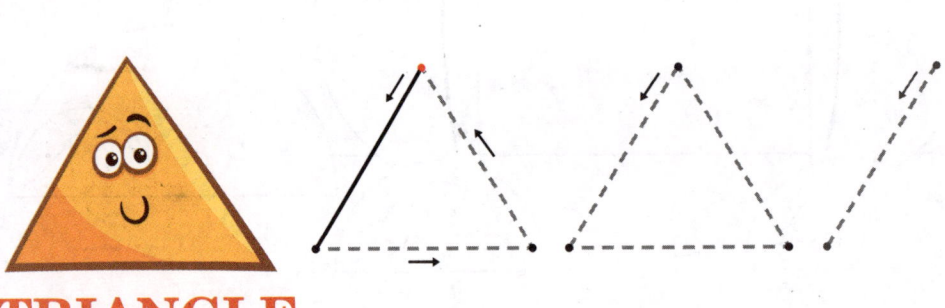

TRIANGLE

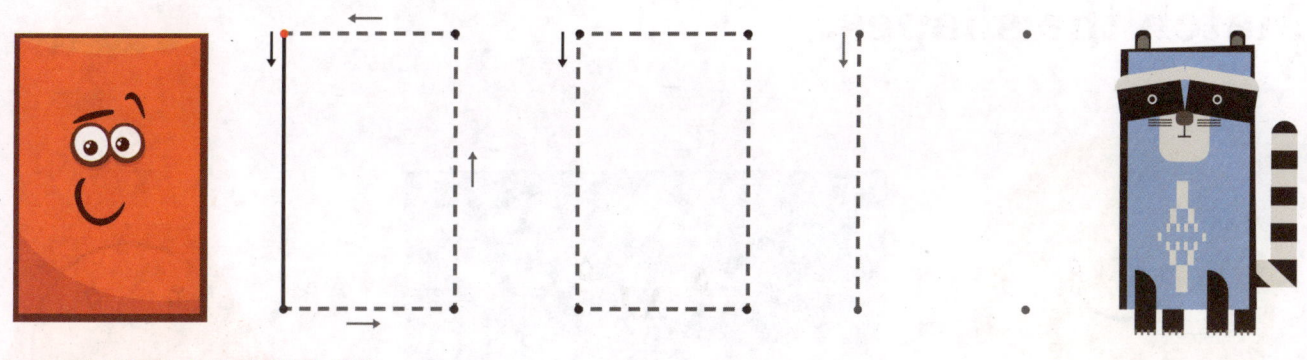
RECTANGLE

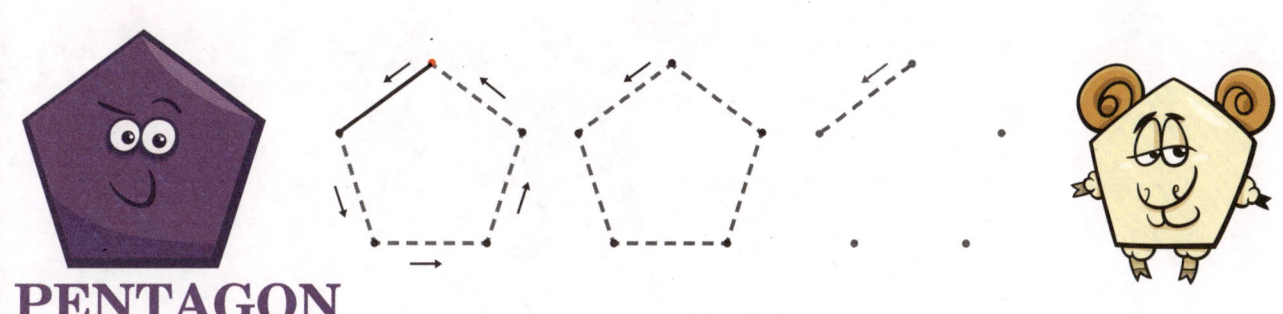
PENTAGON

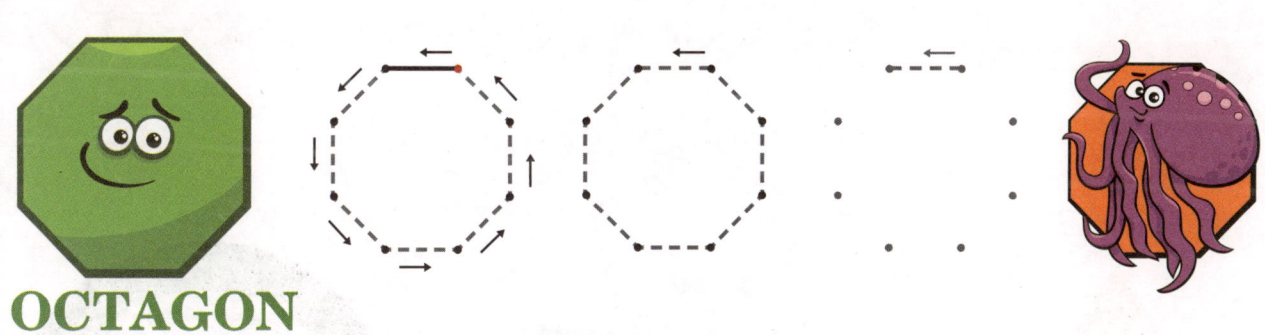
OCTAGON

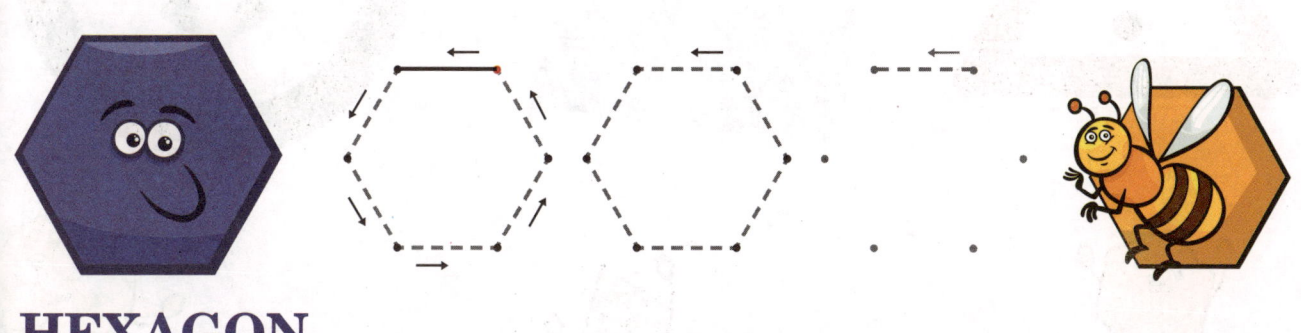
HEXAGON

23

Match the shapes.

25

Match the shadows of the given shapes.

Colour the shape that is the smallest in size in each row.

Which shapes can you identify in the picture? Colour the shapes according to the given colour key.

Colour key

Match the geometric shapes with the shapes of the objects.

Mark the objects in the shape of a circle with an arrow (→).

How many circles can you identify in the given picture? Tick mark (✓) all the circles.

Look at the objects carefully. They resemble geometric shapes. Draw a line to match them with the correct shape.

Help each shape find its house.

Identify the shapes and match them with the correct half.

How many shapes can you find? Count and write your answer.

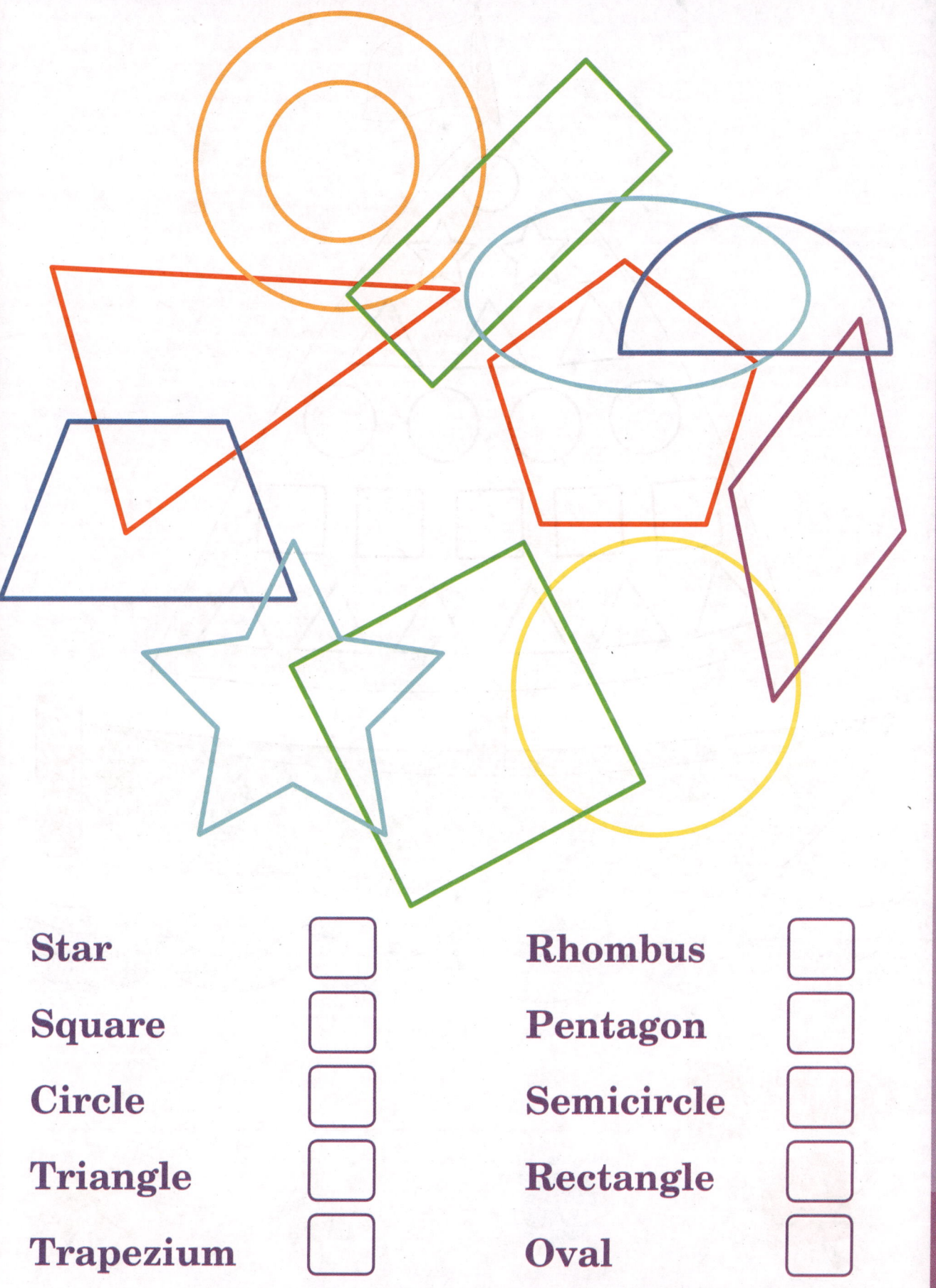

Star	☐	Rhombus	☐
Square	☐	Pentagon	☐
Circle	☐	Semicircle	☐
Triangle	☐	Rectangle	☐
Trapezium	☐	Oval	☐

Colour the shapes according to the given colour key.

Colour key

Match the shapes with the correct shadow.

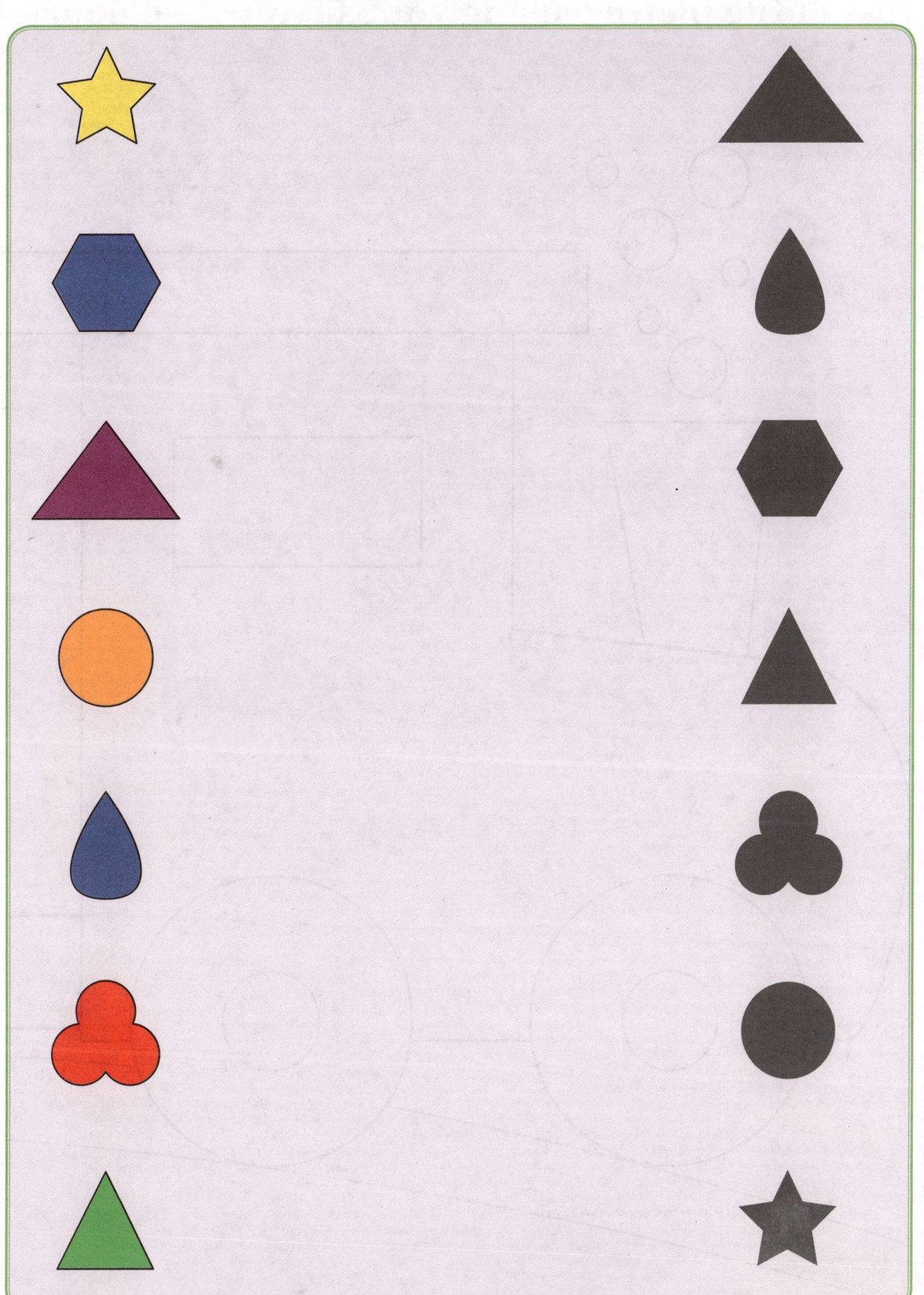

Identify and colour the circles blue. Colour the rest of the picture using your favourite colours.

Let us practice some more shapes. Trace the dots and colour the shapes.

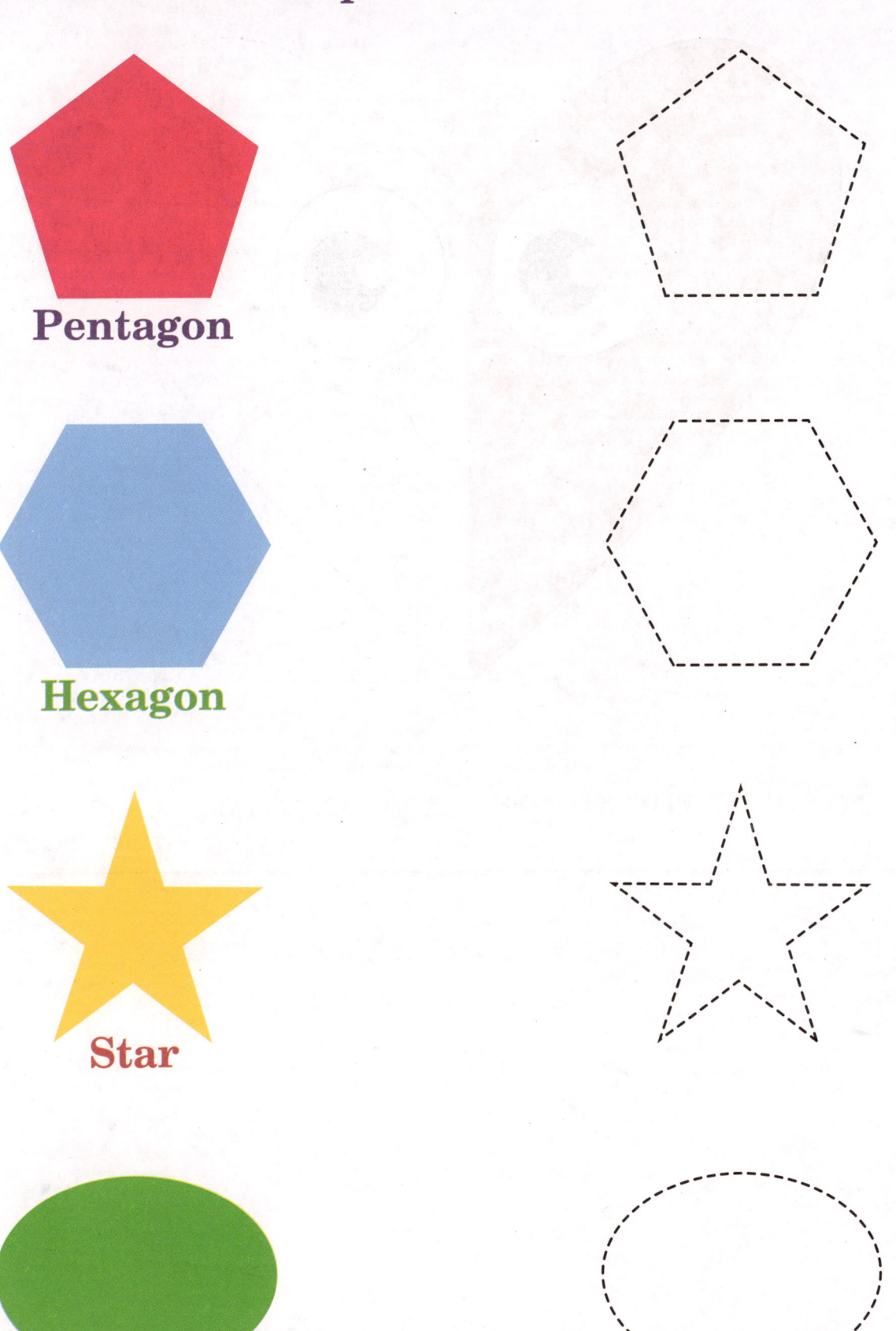

Pentagon

Hexagon

Star

Oval

Heart

Trace the dots and colour the heart shape.

Try to draw the shape on your own.

40

Identify and colour the heart shapes in the picture below.

Help the little triangle to find his way out of the maze.

Hint: Only the triangle doors can be opened.

Match the objects with similar shapes

43

The little circle is lost. Help it find its way out of the maze.

Hint: Only the circle doors can be opened.

Identify and count the similar shapes. Write the answer in the space provided.

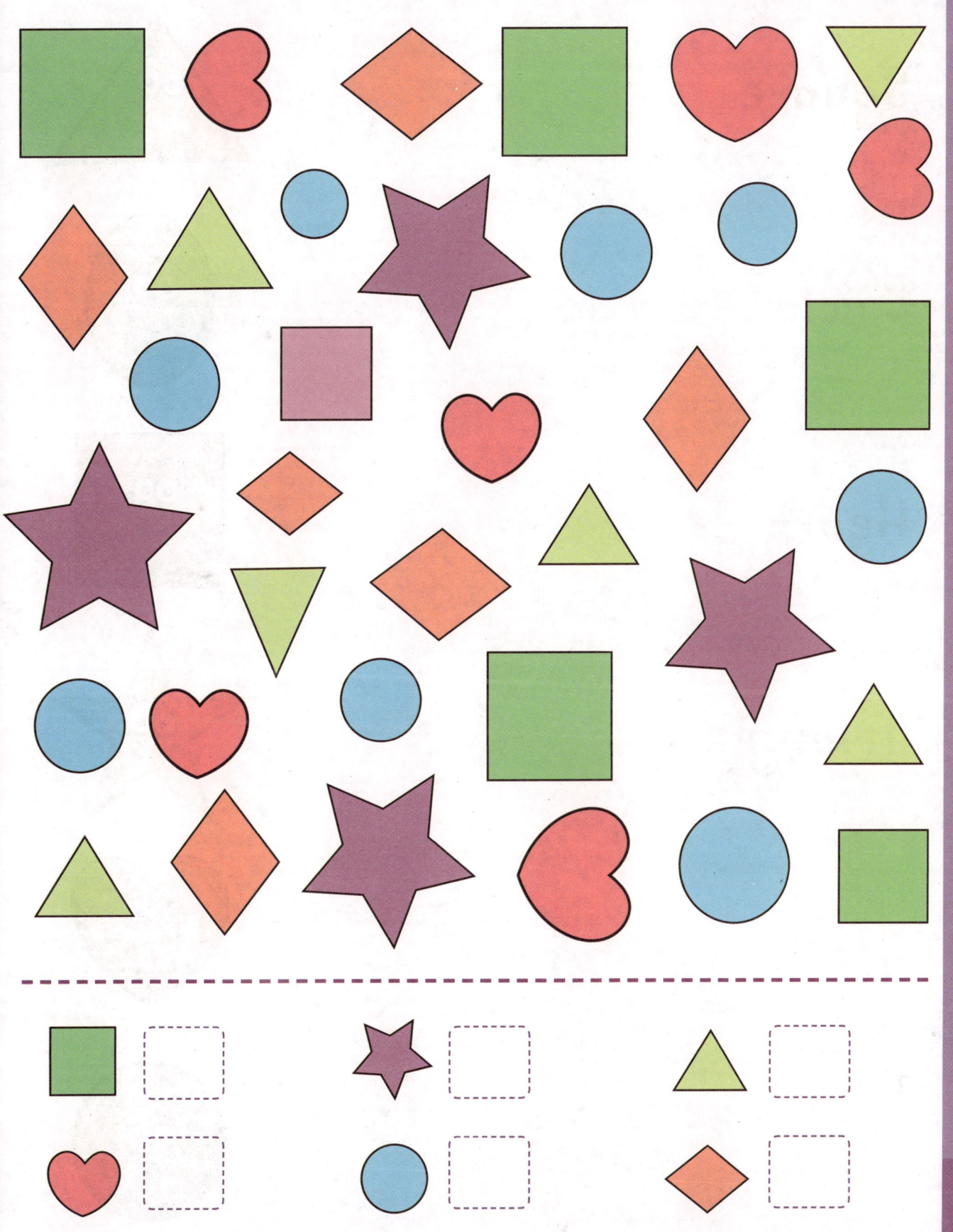

Draw a line and match the shapes with their correct names.

Square

Circle

Heart

Triangle

Oval

Star

Colour the picture according to the colour key provided.

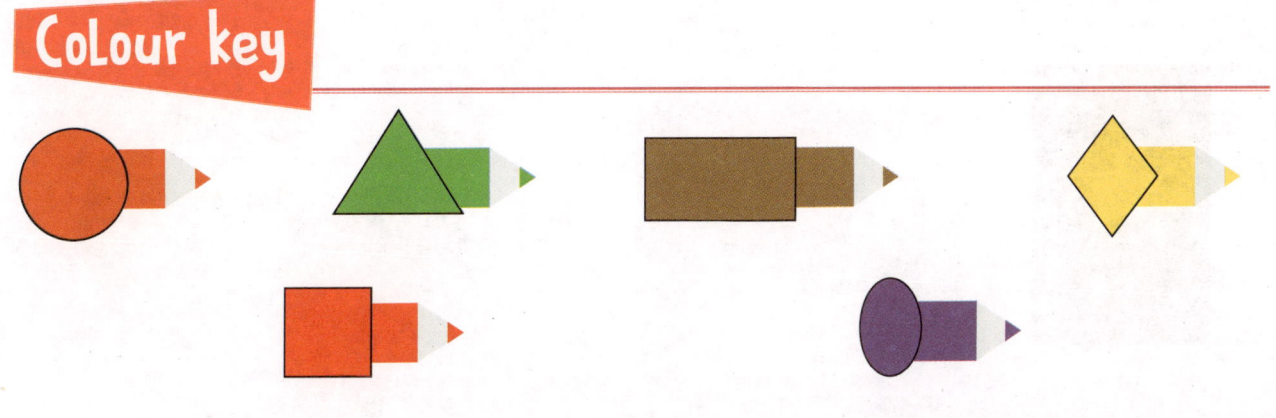

Colour key

Find the right key to open the lock. Draw a line to match the key with the right lock.

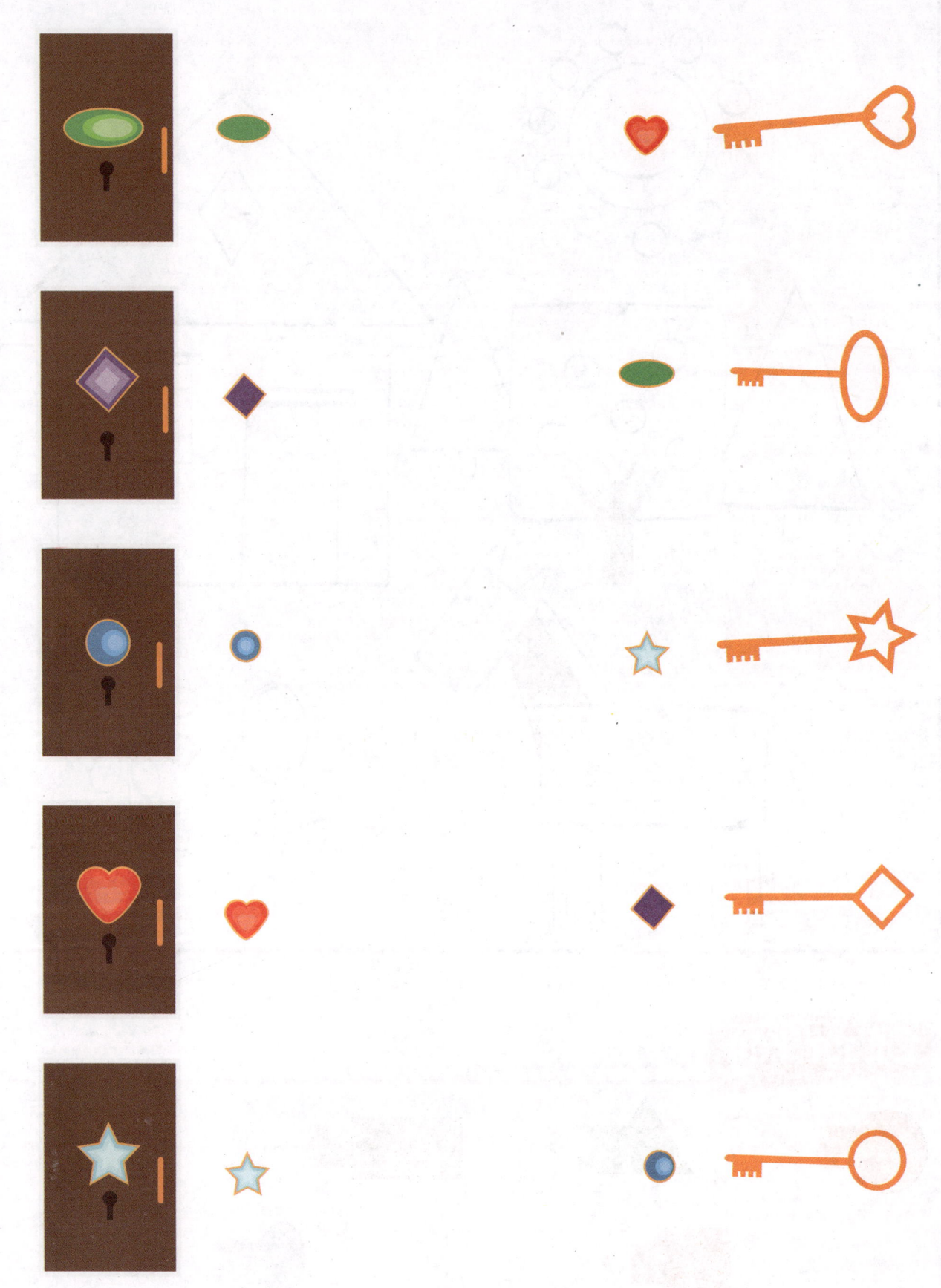

How many squares do you see in the picture? Count and write in the space provided.

Help the little square to find its way out of the maze.

Hint: Only the square doors can be opened

Colour and count the shapes according to the given colour key.

Colour key

Match the objects with the similar shapes.

Find the shapes and colour them according to the colour key.

Colour key

Can you think of some objects around you that look like these shapes? Draw one or more objects for each shape.

Complete the shape Sudoku. Draw and colour the missing shapes. (Each shape should come only once in each row and column.)

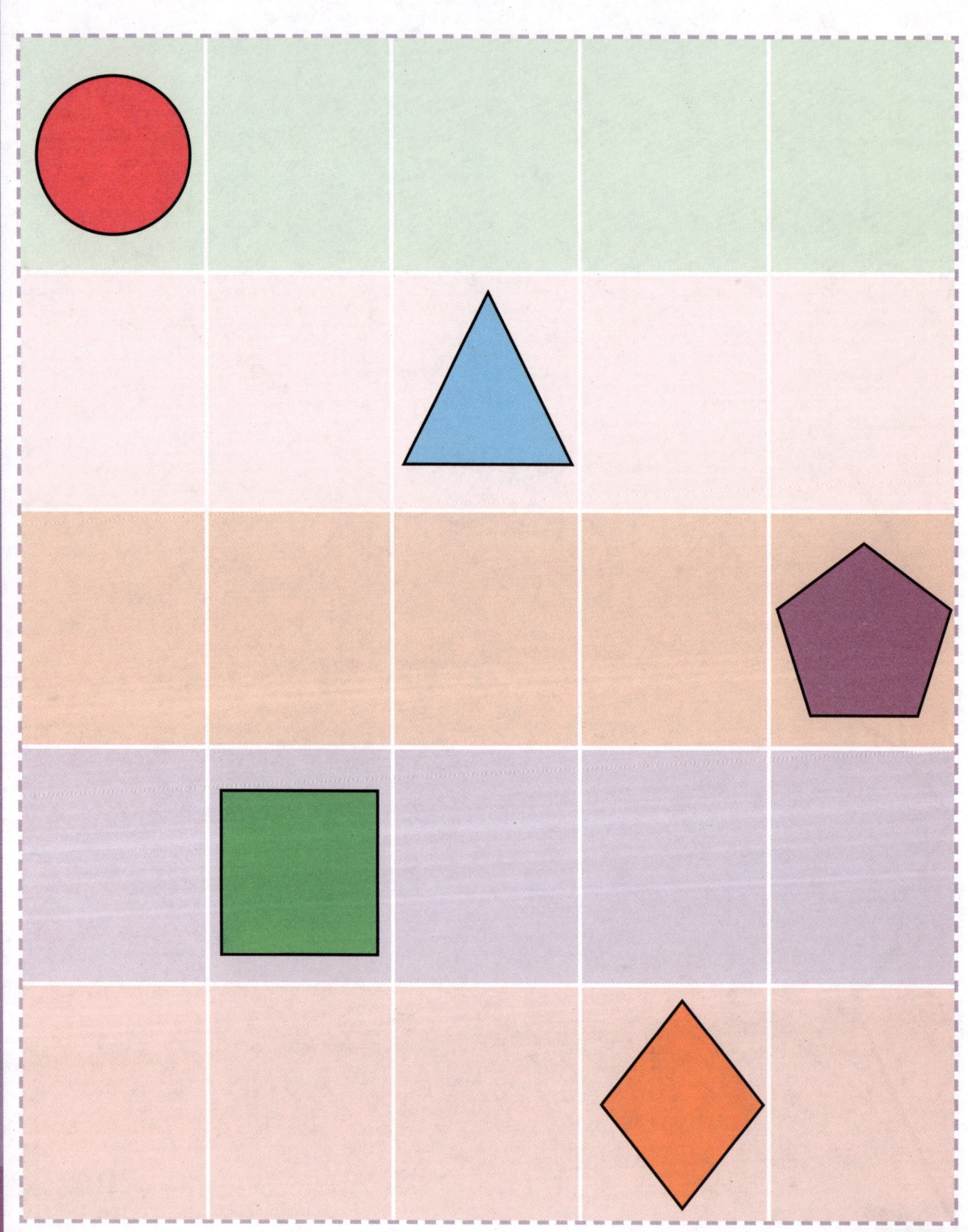

Use the shape colour key and colour the image.

Trace the shape and colour the camel.

Look at the rabbit. Now identify the shapes used to make the rabbit and colour them.

Practice

We have learned about so many shapes! Let' see if you can trace and colour the shapes neatly.

Practice and make shapes by tracing the dots. Also, colour the shapes.

Identify the shapes from the colour key and colour the chick.

64